Praise for *An Abundance of Caution*

An Abundance of Caution is a polyphonic symphony. Moments of meditative observation are followed seamlessly by catharsis while simultaneously drawing readers into a vortex that sometimes forces them to face their own most unsettling instincts. From the observation that during pandemic lockdown "Rush hour ends without a toll of corpses," to the deceptive serenity of a deadly tailing pond, to the cyclical nature of our complacency versus climate change and mass extinction, to a harrowingly surreal conclusion of a poem about a slow day of fishing, this book will challenge, unsettle, and expand its audience's world. I found myself each day looking forward to what new revelations these finely crafted gems of poems would offer up. This is a collection for the ages, one I will keep coming back to again and again.

Anton Yakovlev

Composed during the pandemic, George Witte's latest poems emerge from those lean years keenly aware of the world's frailties and of our own. Threats we have weathered have left their marks: "Infection. Hemorrhage. // Heart fibrillating on the windowsill: / systole absent diastole. // Cool shadow cast, withdrawn. / A sense of something immanent but gone." Realist, elegiac, and deftly musical, *An Abundance of Caution* takes stock of America now, from the vantage point of Witte's native Garden State. His are often hard truths, but like the songbirds in "The Boathouse Swallows," which elude the owner's defenses, Witte's poems find their way in, taking up residence in the mind and heart.

David Yezzi

The poems in George Witte's new book offer intelligent, well-crafted dispatches from a world in which we've learned to live with "an abundance of caution" because of Covid, climate change, environmental devastation, and other calamities. The poems, however, balance elegiac despair with hope for a better future. They remind us that, despite the fact that "storefront pastors blare apocalypse," and despite the fear that humans might "exterminate / creation," we can still enjoy mysterious moments of grace.

Henry Hart

The carefully crafted poems in George Witte's *An Abundance of Caution* are always alert to the subtleties and possibilities of language. Images spring to life, as when plastic bags caught in winter trees "like thought balloons recall / so many empty hands and what they held." A home newly on the market is a "ghost ship uncaptained by disease," suffering "slow mutinies of stuff, / Ash-pocked couch, bottom-broken chair / compressed by bridge and cocktail Saturdays." Witte offers an unflinching glimpse at personal and global degeneration, the "undiagnosed collapse," the summer "the hottest since, more arid than, the worst." It is through these harrowing moments — including a poem titled "The Harrower" — that Witte surprises and startles, so that "we might learn astonishment / again."

Ernest Hilbert

Abundance of caution? Hardly! The first section of the book reminded me strongly of the late Franz Wright's final poems, where he distilled a lifetime of anguish — and dare I say power and victory — in short bursts of truth. Precisely the same feeling hit me here, with each metaphor, each sequence of thought appearing extremely hard-won, involving deep personal sacrifice: "And when undone or desperate, alone / beset by others' hungers and my own / to speak inaudibly and still be heard," as he says in "Wish List." I wondered if Witte could sustain the intensity of the first section's climactic spiritual struggle, and if he should even try. But he manages the rhythm like a master in the succeeding sections, the first of which deals with traces of environmental doom evident in suburbia: "Storefront pastors blare apocalypse / and grin, verses splayed like rodent skins," in "Touch and Go." In the final two sections, he first faces fear and mortality alone, and then returns to family and company but not the universal community represented in the earlier social breakdown. His astute pacing results in certain odd but very welcome readings, such as the opening portion of personal calamity feeling much more tragic than the communal apocalypse that follows. It takes more than one reading to appreciate the symmetry between the "cemetery geese" and "boathouse swallows" in the concluding part, representing the ending and beginning of life respectively. Each poem in this book is to be savored for its deft skillfulness, and almost every phrase has surprises that require mental adjustments. It is a pleasure, a challenge, and a reward to immerse oneself in these highly imaginative poems, each with a strong moral core binding it unbreakably. Witte may perhaps be a poet's poet still, but there is no reason why he shouldn't have a vast audience.

Anis Shivani

George Witte's *An Abundance of Caution* proves Simone Weil's assertion that "We know by means of our intelligence that what the intelligence does not comprehend is more real than what it does comprehend." In poem after poem here, Witte detects what is "half-seen / but known in full embodiment," so that the whole collection is suffused with a "sense of something immanent but gone." *Visionary* is what I would call the quality that enables these poems to know realities that exceed comprehension, to offer the reader "so many empty hands and what they held."

H. L. Hix

Previous Praise for George Witte

Does She Have a Name?

"Witte has done something extraordinary here. At once terrifying and heartrending, *Does She Have a Name?* demonstrates unflinchingly that what lies at the heart of faith is love. It is a great and important work."

Frank Wilson, *Philadelphia Inquirer*

"Witte takes on the subjects of family, medical practice, and physical difference, as a participant witness to tragedy ... In its best moments, the formalism of Witte's verse heightens its emotional resonance ... In a poem about revisiting his living will during a period of extreme uncertainty, the final, formal lines create a beautiful, ironic tension between bureaucratic tasks and the lives they sustain: "Asleep, our issue shudders in your arms. / I sign in triplicate against more harm."

Kirkus Reviews

Deniability

"Witte's achievement rests in maintaining his poise and applying his considerable intelligence even in the heat of the national moment ... this collection stands a chance of enduring as a work of witness."

American Book Review

"George Witte's *Deniability* takes on the war on terror, chronicling the myriad ways in which, with language as accomplice, it has left "the mind's-eye map ... undone." In verse forms attuned to contain a flyaway reality, Witte relentlessly deconstructs the host of verbal misappropriations such as "hearts and minds," "just war," "rendition," and "friendly fire" that blindside political discourse and with every repetition are "pearled anew." Beginning with the fall of the Twin Towers and traveling forward in time, *Deniability* tracks an America enthralled by images of violence and fear. The deeply ironic voice of many of the poems is that of "we the people," whose government's power "to crush again and kiss the damage" enslaves both other nations and ourselves."

Lee Sharkey, author of *A Darker, Sweeter String*

"That arch-citizen, Suspicious, who lived among Them in the Cold War, now lives among Us. Is Us now. We all feel the costs and compromises of living ordinary lives in a nation whose actions contradict its ideals, but naming those costs and compromises (the first step toward contesting them) is difficult when our linguistic well has been poisoned by pervasive lying. That is why, now as ever, now more than ever, we need poetry, and it is the challenge George Witte's *Deniability* accepts. From its first word, "uh-oh," to its last, "listen," *Deniability* shows us — commuters in "the tattooed N or R train / Eeling underground" — our lives, tenders us that clarity the absence of which "dispossesses our heirs by / failing," as our leaders and media have failed, "to record the deed."

H. L. Hix, National Book Award finalist, author of *Chromatic*

"Smart, timely, and sane, this volume is highly recommended."

Library Journal **(Wilda Williams)**

"*Deniability* is a book that begins with disasters and disorientations and moves through various tensions towards a questioning of witness, particularly photography. Formally held but lightly at an angle, the movement of the verse is sharp and a little purposively jerky, as though the whole world were on edge, the writing now dense and compressed, now clean like an open highway. There is always the option of tight control but options remain open. It is the tensions of our time George Witte is articulating and singing into shape. As he says: "Every corner / seems another threshold, as though / you carry something delicate / from block to block toward home ..."

George Szirtes, author of *Reel*

The Apparitioners

"*The Apparitioners* is George Witte's first book of poetry, but you would never guess it from his confident, ironic style, which moves easily from colloquial speech-rhythms to rich natural description ... Like a Frost of the suburbs, Mr. Witte regards the cozy, domesticated landscape he inhabits with an unsettling lucidity, which gives everything he sees the aspect of a parable or a warning ... Anyone who has felt intimations of mortality in our American abundance will recognize the power of Mr. Witte's poems."

Adam Kirsch, *New York Sun*

Set among suburban homes and in neighboring forests and fields, Witte's descriptive verse, seasonal lyric and short narrative poems arrive in sonnets, in all manner of rhyming stanzas and in meticulous free verse. This debut collection describes the "Frail correspondences / Required of mass and air / To lift the hawk" into flight; treats the fears of parents in "cul-de-sacs"; considers October sparrows in "fall's / false spring"; and compares the speaker and his friends to fireflies, who "pass in time from form to form, / containers for a glow not ours." Witte's interest in casual American speech, and some of his Northeastern landscapes, suggest Robert Frost, while the austerity of his diction, and his more than passing interest in mortality, imply lessons learned from Anthony Hecht. His search for human lesson in gardens and fields, and his attraction to green retreats, even suggests Frost's sometime model Horace, who propounded worldly wisdom from his Sabine farm. Witte, who is editor-in-chief of St. Martin's Press, concludes with a dramatic monologue, written in the voice of a woman recovering (slowly) from a stroke; it wings slowly from urgent pathos to a kind of bitter resignation, and works to balance the more contented voices that carry the shorter poems. The calm fortitude the latter display suggest work of long planning and considered judgment: Horace himself might approve.

Publishers Weekly

"A genuine religious sensibility informs these poems, animated not by allegiance to doctrines, rituals, or commands, but rather by a sense of mystery ... If you read only one book of poems this year, make it this one."

Frank Wilson, *Philadelphia Inquirer*

"Mature in both voice and vision ... The nature lyric is the art at which he excels, eschewing the traps of ego and shaping crystalline detail with the motion of thought in a style that evokes both A. R. Ammons and Robert Frost ... There is much to recommend here."

Wilda Williams, *Library Journal*

" ... a serious and impressive debut ... Reviewers have made comparisons between Witte and Frost; it seems too, that he shares some of Amy

Clampitt's proclivity for lush language, some of Larkin's wry cynicism ... I was impressed by the sense of craft, patience, and vision."

Jessica Murray, *Birmingham Poetry Review*

"George Witte is a metaphysician of the suburbs, alert to the heights and depths that inhere in everyday life ... This is a lovely, auspicious debut."

Willard Spiegelman

"Out of the shared wounds and joys, the inner weather and the outer, the world we live in and the one we dream about, George Witte makes poems that are marked by a rare clarity and accessibility."

George Garrett

"George Witte's intensity of intelligence burns down scenes to their forms, perceiving a play of mischief and meaning in the marvelously ordinary. He is the best kind of formalist, a Stevensonian sort for whom paradigms emerge from randomness ... His linguistic glow, around a larger patterning, is rare and original. Read him."

James Applewhite

"*The Apparitioners* presents a complex but bracingly clear view of a world where apparent ease and security are undermined by apprehension, by a certain but undefined knowledge that forces dark and deep are destroying the underpinnings of contemporary life ... Here is a remarkable achievement, thoughtful, skillful, and above all, original. Here is a volume that will be admired — and trusted."

Fred Chappell

An Abundance of Caution

An Abundance of Caution

George Witte

UNBOUND EDITION PRESS

Atlanta

Copyright © 2023 by George Witte
All Rights Reserved

FIRST EDITION

Printed in the United States of America

LIBRARY OF CONGRESS RECORD

Name: Witte, George, 1960– author.
Title: An Abundance of Caution / George Witte.
Edition: First edition.
Published: Atlanta : Unbound Edition Press, 2023.

LCCN: 2022942476
LCCN Permalink: https://lccn.loc.gov/2022942476
ISBN: 978-0-9913780-6-7 (hardcover)

Designed by Eleanor Safe and Joseph Floresca
Printed by Bookmobile, Minneapolis, MN
Distributed by Small Press Distribution

123456789

Unbound Edition Press
1270 Caroline Street, Suite D120
Box 448
Atlanta, GA 30307

"Bodies have their own light which they consume to live: they burn, they are not lit from the outside."

Egon Schiele

Contents

I. Trestle Jumping

Trestle Jumping	23
Host	24
Easter Candles	25
Who What When Where Why	27
Overheard	28
Confinement	29
Bellfounding	30
Nymphs	31
Prodigal	33
Wish List	34
Reap	35
Verge	36
The Swing of Things	37
The Virgin of Perth Amboy	38
Found	39

II. An Abundance of Caution

The Hall of Human Origins	42
Back of the Napkin	44
Birdfall	45
Prey Abundance	46
Empties	48
Tailing Pond	49
Flash to Bang	50
On That Happy Note	51
If/Then	52
Been There Done That	53
Touch and Go	54
Carriers	55
Sprinklers	57
Our Heart Goes Out	58
An Abundance of Caution	60
After the Recent Unpleasantness	61

III. The Underpass

Search	64
For the Foreseeable	65
Migration	66
Apnea	68
Easy Way Out	69
The Harrower	70
The Way Back	72
The Plunge Pool	73
What Doesn't Kill You	74
The Hatch	76
Process of Elimination	77
Theirs	78
The Angler	80
I	82
Friends and Acquaintances	83
Whereabouts Unknown	84
Darkling	85
Exit Interview	86

IV. As Is

Totems	88
Nightlight	90
Scab	91
Afield	92
Rise	94
Lighting Up	95
Night Swimming	97
Bearing Wall	98
Visiting Hours	100
Cemetery Geese	102
As Is	104
The Boathouse Swallows	106

An Abundance
of Caution

I. Trestle Jumping

Trestle Jumping

Chains barricade the gravel exit ramp
our bankrupt state abandoned years ago.
Unlatched, the way descends to miles of road
invisible on maps, near overgrown,
eroded where low water tunnels through.
Lights out we race pitch lanes between faint lines,
full moon our sightless, disembodied guide.
Only those who don't fear dying drive. Eyes
wild or cool, no-one eases off or brakes
before the trestle bridge, graffitied span
a palimpsest of wills and testaments.
GODBOY   DOA   XXRIP
Inebriate but sobered up we strip
to briefs, cinch bungee cords around slick waists
and climb the piton-studded vertical.
Each handhold ratchets up a body's length
until we reach the overpass, fix rope
around protruding rebar and prepare.
A radio suggests alternatives:
Be like they are...we'll be able to fly.
Step off and try embracing air, our screams
the secret names of all who sang in kind.

Host

devour me as you were devoured
before recorded history

release me as you were released
breathed in again   molecular

forgive me as you were forgiven
life   and lived unmade   unseen

we know each other well enough
to violate proprieties

fillet me   burn and blacken   tear
limb from limb as you were torn

by implements intelligence
deploys to render fear or shame

synonymous with you   the name
no father weighs upon his son

answer doubt with evidence
as you did mine   rude trafficker

in rags   invisible until
one table lamp ignited

every bowl and dull utensil
gold   astonishing your host

nothing comes between us   air
light   forget me as you were

Easter Candles

    Dutiful but faithless,
        hypocrisy suburbanized,
I lightly doze through alleluia rounds.

    Unfamiliar tourists
        mime greeting and reply, this day
occasion for a dressy brunch, no more.

Devout parishioners find pews,
pine bowed from centuries of restless glutes.
        Tall windows cracked for air

admit insinuating song, the birds'
        old hymn of earth delivered by
                Persephone's return.

    A sounding bowl rings silence in;
        our minister ascends.
To lighten sorrows and exalt small joys

    three candles stand alone,
        heights ranged as if suggesting time.
Their quietus invokes remembrances;

    shades gather one by one, aloud
        or summoned silently,
passed on or born, beset or well, the names

like sleepers freed from kingdoms under spell.
    The homily begins.
   Lacunae in Luke's narrative

   disable gravity:
Fraught women prone before an empty tomb,
   two desert travellers, a third

who questions certain marvellous events
   while feigning human ignorance.
     With broken bread reveals

   himself as dusk descends, half-seen
but known in full embodiment, then gone.
    The candles flutter low,

    reluctant, aged, frail.
The congregation seems to hold its breath.
   Each flame consumes itself, but stays.

Who What When Where Why

Necks bow in unison,
alone.
       At church or phone
in urgent prayer, awaiting
word: when and where
dread happens.
              What.
                     An egret —
rapt, infallible —
spreads wings to shadow
water calm and draw
reluctant minnows near,
                the way
lost palmers huddle under trees from storm despite
strike risk, while ruptured light
stabs down. And if such shade
seems grace, though false,
then who knows otherwise
or why?

Overheard

The silenced coalesce within
    disturbances of air.
Ascending ladderways of rain
    they hasten everywhere:

Abandoned nests in winter trees,
    high eave or tunnelled mound,
safe anchorage for refugees
    run merciless to ground.

But listening between the din
    of transit and delay,
long lulls in conversation when
    one hesitates to say

the unrepentant shibboleth,
    frail secret couched in flame,
I hear them whisper under breath
    and recognize my name.

Confinement

At the exhibition,
long lines shuffle close to pause
before this child.
Her painted face half-turns away,
calm within our hungry gaze,
flesh nascent, pale and full
beneath the simple shift
one candle gilds.
The room or cell is windowless —
narrow bed and chair,
whittled figurine
to which she kneels —
each corner thick where motes
revolve in slow suspense, a question
answered by her name.
She cannot know the quickening
that keeps her here,
what will arrive or when.
The candle traces
faint blue veins along her wrists,
arm-hair sprung against damp chill,
livid scar
transecting one clasped hand
a word that only she
endures the meaning of.

Bellfounding

In steepled space we quietly conspire
my waist and lip surround your tongue
indwelling   calm and reticent   it's time
by wheel and pulley made to sway
are sounded   rung   but fractured through
each day   beyond repair until
the secret furnace of communion smelts
dross down to elements   slow-cooled   cast new
our flaw no longer silences
now sings and summons congregants who flock
beneath dew-heavy elms in finery
to crowded aisles where absence   is
contained like oxygen   or light
refracting humid colonnades of dust
all rise to offer willing voice   still un-
aware they keep such fervent company

Nymphs

They come
less often now, watchful with unease,
in camouflage where once
their secret beds and alibis
were vouchsafed me.

                        One stepped
on tentative soft hooves,
alert and delicate, then flew
two bounds across the verge
between our kind. Another
calmly sang in unfamiliar tongue
so close my skin
became a bell of shy assent.
And when the frozen lake gave way
to early April thaw
the groans of ruptured ice were breath
compressed and held, as I
held mine, surrendering.

                        Today
I find what then seemed mystery,
still clutched into an oak:
cicada carapace, a perfect caul.
I hold it to the sun,
blind scientist, squint wise
as if by darkened gaze I see,

then toss it down unrecognized.
But in my palm
the relic pricks, each lobe
a livid brand, and though I rub
astounded by such pain,
erasing trace,
it will not fade.

Prodigal

The universe makes paperwork of stars,
aligning messy desk and calendar,

mail emptied for tonight. No end but churn,
expand and die, beyond intelligence.
Heads back some gape in fields, or taking turns

around the calm dark pond imagine they
are seen, reflected in another eye.

A flare descends: misdriven chariot,
debris to puncture humid paradise.
Lost relative disowned by secret vote

who gently asks *Do you remember when?*
while fathers stare in grave bewilderment.

Wish List

To travel light, a spider vaulting air.

To lean through shadow, synthesize enough
from fallen things. To thrive but not devour.

Adhere.   Indwell.   Emerge from carapace.
Reveal the awful secret kept between
initiates, foretelling and foretold.

Within debris, to see geometry.

As if another being entered mine,
erasing memory and tongue, to move
through stations of release until the pain
becomes a current flowing deep and cold.

Unseen, to occupy a property
as is, without intent to dispossess.

To say goodbye before the path descends.

In altered form to go unrecognized
among conspirators and kin. Forgive
apologies and touch affliction clean,
embodiment of dust and light, as breath
exhaled in autumn plumes, then dissipates.

And when undone or desperate, alone,
beset by others' hungers and my own,
to speak inaudibly and still be heard.

Reap

We sing what we have sown   low voices hushed
in hope and shame before whatever ear
might listen in   excuses salting praise
as meat is seasoned to devour   as we
devour our kind   forgiveness sought but not
required by covenant   to each his own
to each alone the terror quickening
who knows when the wind began to summon
strength and turn around its thermal axis
made great by our debris and dust   where we
conceal most secret selves it touches down
in basement   shelter   roadside ditch   we learn
the word's embedded anagrams   so rush
to pare a god's indifferent nails and rape
the body offered in all innocence
and gnaw the hanging unripe pear of love

Verge

They sidle close
at dusk, across
our street or hovering
next door. A sill between
still air and wind, as when
my heart withholds one beat —
dead time — but soon repeats
it: grace, again.

Or flow below
an open grate
for those who come and go
because they're needed home,
if only for a day.
Shadow at the threshold.
Spring welling cold
from underground,

behind drywall
where nests abide —
they sidle close, surround
intangibles with light.
All skins ignite, return
as particles, exhaled
yet taken in;
so I am held.

The Swing of Things

A goldfinch grips the sunflower's
    lean stalk, which bows
  beneath each failed ascent,
    corolla seeds
  serene beyond its beak.
Clenched claws inch down, then up again,
    persistent supplicant
      for grace withheld,
head checking side to side in case
    rapaciously observed.
    It's only me,
I whisper from the windowpane
in witness and conspiracy.
    The dance continues, rapt
with appetite denied until,
    surrendering,
it stitches off in dips and starts
    to richer realms. The stalk
    finds equilibrium
      and stands erect,
frail lever set to pull and whirl
    enfolded parallels,
      star within star,
      cell within cell
    sustained by fine array,
the swing of things inhering in
    and under all.

The Virgin of Perth Amboy

A ground floor rental unit beckons us,
devout, amused, or merely curious.
Reporters prowl the crush, interrogate
credulity, take addresses and names.
Crowds overwhelm the town police, clog streets
with Chryslers, Harleys, station wagons, Fords,
umbrellas spread against the sun. Polite,
respectful of each other's privacy
we gather near, mute witnesses into
the window where her features coalesce,
reluctant eyes cast down to chasten pride.
Dad points the Instamatic lens and clicks.
Mom lights a Camel, squinting through the pall.
No docent volunteers the protocol:
How long to wait until kids wander off,
demanding ice cream and balloons before
her apparition's likely to resume,
late afternoon as shadows deepen space
or when the washer/dryer's steam ascends.
It's unconfirmed, ambiguous, depends —
who knows? One woman claims she doesn't show
unless you say her name, then sidle eyes
aside, as if to calm an animal.
At last we funnel through a maze of rope
that barricades the modest entryway;
heads bowed, approach on hands and knees to touch
one squared-off pane, impress damp fingerprints,
commingled oils a veil through which we see
ourselves transfigured by the darkened glass
and apprehend what cannot be explained.

Found

From topsoil-dampened knees
I summon idols quietly:
    Bird and animal, small

familiars that abide nearby
    or dwell undeified
        in nests beneath my skin.

They are not false, but secret kin,
    approach with watchful care,
        pretend I'm theirs.

    Forget their given names
that we might learn astonishment
again, restored by touch the way

    afflicted beggars were.
My open hands char raw where light
        incinerates.

    Come cardinal,
      low flame against spring snow;
I know your call and hideaway.

Come deer in delicate parade;
      soft lips devour
        my every bud.

And should you find me disarrayed,
    unkempt from intercourse
    consensual, if strange,

do not prepare or purify
    my rude material
        with herbs and oil

    but let me broken lie
    in state, anonymous,
no graven stone to find me by.

II. An Abundance of Caution

The Hall of Human Origins

From awful beasts by meteor extinct
I shuffle past familiar skulls:
Restored assemblages of shard and paste,
grave ancestors. The darkened hall
pools whispers deep, archaic undercroft
where doubt and fear enkindle praise
before remains approximating God.
Ineffable, their skeletons
more child than fully grown; thick-browed, long limbs
evolved to climb and hunt. One hip
reveals bipedal ease, notched socket bone
that braced the spine and muscle mass
when some emerged from trees to face or flee
new predators. This fossil track
preserves their nascent gait, as two decamped
through falling ash four million years
ago, in panorama looking back:
volcanic fire and lava flow,
Uriel blazing at the garden gate,
bush scorched like cities of the plain.
Compressed in river mud small footprints blend
with other animals' quartets,
enormous hooves and claw-tipped paws among
the twin anomalies, who ran
for lives here pieced together with surmise.

Unmanned, embarrassing myself
with tears, I mumble names of absences.
Our line diminishes behind,
trail overgrown, inheritance picked clean.
Sue, Eva, Aunt Ruth and Edna,
Nick, Robert, Rose and Richard, Peg and George.
By length of stride and depth of heel
I guess departure speed but cannot know
their exile's origin or end.

Back of the Napkin

Assuming seven years   the balance
tips   both poles collapse so
oceans fall like hungry ghosts
upon our grain and property
then figure fifty give or
take's when nothing stays   sun
surveilling what it lasers off
infernos roam the highland   ridge
to vale   through empty neighborhoods
downhill   downtown   for eras more
bombarded cells divide and multiply
maybe we'll evolve   made new
sprout embryonic tail and gills
no ears   we've heard enough
no language to advantage us
cornered by the foaming verge
our last resort   this ark
of sand   bears vagrant refugees
escaping time   roach and scorpion
kangaroo and rat   sea black
with ash against our backs
we face the fire   voice
great with wind   and whisper
god   or cry out   *mommy*
find me   *pull me in*

Birdfall

We rarely find them   fallen   soft
intruders desecrating lawns
as if they might awaken   kissed
from spell   by fruit or needle's prick
imprisoned on another plane
in parallel   like specimens
or photographs of missing kids
one's disquiet   two alarm   three
the breach between their world and our
unvaccinated realm   before
we know what's hit us it evolves
a hive outsmarting remedy
no prayer avails   nowhere to hide
away   authorities collect
each one with Hazmat suits and probes
to map the rate of imminence
and once upon a time   a boy
found blackening the neighbor's wood
a stricken flock on rigorous
parade   sharp yellow beaks agape
distended tongues and wings wrenched loose
by mindful hands still lingering
invisible nearby   he called
for help but couldn't whisper loud
enough for anyone to hear

Prey Abundance

Brazen chipmunks shred our front porch pumpkins.
Flying squirrels colonize the attics,
rats garages, geese the bustling graveyard

where yesterday we sank another friend.
Absent predators, the balance falters;
by choice or chance or fearful quarantine
we've let things go. No grinning fox and kits

prance confident from yard to yard, nor do
red-shouldered hawks nest grandly in an oak,
their baleful presence quelling every song.

Rush hour ends without a toll of corpses.
And mornings lengthen into afternoons
as watching for the brindle cat I mourn
its patient audience. Familiarly

yet strange it held my eye as kin know kin,
lapped milk set out to pacify the fates
then, muscles supple under tawny skin

elided through the underbrush to chase
peculiar appetites. Bewildered, numb
from scotch and forced confinement we forget
such ministry, our sinecure the cull

of weaker prey. Lawns pocked with burrow holes,
these months undo the sanguinary chain,
as if by spell our kingdom were beset,

suspended outside time. On clotted nights
of suffocating dream I ask myself
why childhood years gape blank as calendars,
what did or didn't happen when, and whose

kept secrets deliquesce while stories trail
away unfinished and the answer is-
n't that I don't remember, but I can't.

Empties

December   bags in funerary trees
enkindle when late daylight hastens down
strange foliage   abandoned nests   or souls
disowned   adrift in whirling vortices
no name or broken body to renew
what tore them free from care   breath passing through
invisible but violent as fire
downed limbs and sizzling wires   roof peeled from nails
small husks of animals and birds caught out
once seen they're everywhere   conveying air
in permanent captivity   this month
of star-cast birth and merchandise the bags
bear witness but decline to testify
inhale   collapse   like thought balloons recall
so many empty hands and what they held

Tailing Pond

To birds it glows, ingredients disguised
by shallow water turquoise shading through
degrees of blue to deepest indigo.
Drawn down before they realize

why autumn light refracts in strange array
come migratory geese and swans, wings spread
before descent into a common grave.
Like ruined brides they thrash miswed

to tar that blackens every quill and chokes
once-graceful throats, so cannot warn away
attendant rafts. The pond's unseeing gaze
contains the sky, incurious

as God. No breath disturbs the silent urn.
Its work is slow, the sift of centuries.
No mother will conceive here or return.
It renders pure impurity.

Flash to Bang

Beachgoers eye approaching anvil clouds.
Between the bolt and boom of air displaced
five seconds mark a mile. Like sleepers roused
we stumble over dunes, beg children race,
collapse umbrellas, stumble through dense gloom

for cars. Some brave the swollen firmament,
surf unconcerned through candid diatoms
lit green beneath their graceful boards against
impermanence. As if great claws devein

reluctant seams of light the fabric tears
in dislocating strobe and thunder reigns.
We daven to our superpredator.

Above damp sand trash whirls like restless souls.
Warm humid afterbreath floods ventricles

with suffocating ease. I think we're done.

On That Happy Note

Why bother when no matter what
you'll make the same mistakes again,
abolish graven covenants
and measure hurricane and fire
by loss to personal effects.
Create false paper trails, inter
dissent in unmarked shallow graves.
Squander all except dominion.

In time, green capillary threads
emerge from charred remains, annex
this virgin host of parasites.
Skies clear with your abandonment;
befouled canals run blue and cold.
Expungement fathers wilderness
without permission or complaint.
The working is mysterious.

Unless anyone objects — no? —
continue as before, although
diminished temporarily.
Forgive our trespasses as we,
you whisper when another goes.
Unquiet nights close darker now,
mass emanation dimmed so stars
convene, reoccupying air.

If/Then

Deranged by wind the temple whirls,
adorers pinned or flung.
Ash ruptures the ozonosphere.
Deep ligatures undone.

Despite inventive alibis
the jury has returned.
Beseeching hymn nor sacrifice
avail when mountains burn.

If suggests as barkers do next
try will be the winner.
Then luck descends, made manifest;
prize terrible to bear.

Been There Done That

Imbalances of oxygen:
Too much, the biosphere resets
by one degree, or three,
enough to mass exterminate
creation, land and sea.

Too little kills the largest first,
destroying habitat and plants
they fattened on. Then low
give way to lower orders, ants
then mites, bacteria

at last, from which all things renew.
For eons levels stabilize;
now ozone breathes and holds
us close with whispered lullabies
against the fire and cold

to come again. Each livid day's
a chariot deranged, as when
our forebears watched a seed
of burning mineral descend
yet bent, unmoved, to feed.

Touch and Go

A little dicey now,
no telling where or how
it's headed but it is.
Storefront pastors blare apocalypse
and grin, verses splayed like rodent skins.
Each day more birds collide
with glass, bemused or dead
around the house, their navigation
gone, as if our axis
shifted by degree, one
nudge enough to loosen gravity,
derange the seas that inundating
inch. The city's damp perimeter
erodes, marina swamped, jogging paths
impassable in parts,
asphalt crenellations
stormed and overrun. From the bridge's
elevated prospect it's okay:
We greet each other as if nothing's
happened, raising caffeinated drinks,
escorting dogs — *Hello,*
Let's get together, Great! —
a touch before we go
more profitable ways, whatever
hastens waste or pauses time to make
unmaking it worthwhile.

Carriers

Crushed lilies betray visitors:
Two adults with fawn
bedded down and gone by dawn,
shy lovers gently fleeing ravished ground.
Emerging into secrecy
they soft-shoe through the darkened town
of vacant shops and blinking traffic lights,
ignoring other lawns for ours.
Discriminate and sure
nip buds —
rose, hydrangea, hyssop, phlox —
lick dry the birdbath bowl.

                              Each leg
enacts a covert dance,
high step and pause half-bent, descend
precise around staked mesh,
past motion-triggered floods and pungent sprays
employed for lesser pests.
You ask if we should call authorities.
Like messengers from time they bear
contagion of old plagues
last seen in dimming photographs and painted wood,
soccer fields of bodies burned and bulldozed
deep, wraiths ascending from infected homes.

I preach homeowner's pieties,
bravado trumping expertise.
We'll fasten hats, long sleeves and pants,
gel-sanitize stray hands,
comb scalp and groin for sign
our border's breached, intruders
claiming who and what we own,
malignant or benign,
unshriven or divine,
against which nothing will secure.

Sprinklers

I could rely on rain, as neighbors do,
content with itchy, weed-infested lawns.
One day, the punctured atmosphere
will render measures moot,
Jerusalem made new,
smothering who
extracted, razed, and guzzled every drop.
Seen only by insomniacs
more automated systems hiss awake.
Each head exhales percussive mist
arrayed in dancers' rows
of grave, meticulous ballet.

Tomorrow sun reveals
from stem to bud to deliquescent branch
a fortune strung to vaporize,
bequeathed as air.
Like paradise, or getting there.
I sip black coffee toasting two
crows keen on my demise.
No bees disturb their gustatory view.
Damp pistils go unfertilized.

Our Heart Goes Out

To you and yours
engraved on tasteful stationery, gold
initials framing Shen Zhou's waterfall
above a stony trail
one traveller descends.

                    And shared, of course,
grief riven from the ancient scroll,
search-optimized with **#death** and **#beautiful**
to lure indifferent eyes.

                    For loss
makes strangers bedfellows —
a stricken pet, a loved one's slow demise,
or suicide
by dozens as the case so often is
these trembling days,
across which viscous threads
invisibly connect, expanding with each breath's
malignant kiss.

                    It's difficult to say,
no words express, we can't relate
or offer sincere sympathies,
bring food or babysit, not now,
not soon. Best wishes resonate
like prayers in an empty ear.
We're inconsolable
as you, alone

by fearful choice and dispossessed of sleep,
beside a reading lamp
that like your heart surrenders pace
to fibrillate,
left on too many vagrant, burning nights,
yet slows, mysteriously stayed,
and somehow holds.

An Abundance of Caution

Go watchfully in humid fog
emerging on the first warm day

with skeins of birds and dogs unleashed
to race through greenery, alive.

Proceed as if on shattered glass
around suspicious passersby

eyeing each other's mask and gloves,
give way or cross the street devoid

of traffic, nowhere to commute,
on holiday but isolate.

Immunity begets a herd
evolving to cooperate,

walled colony insured against
collapse until the barrier

erodes with mutability,
the slow or sudden shift awry

that ravins every virgin cell.
Before a cenotaph of shoes

abandoned to the elements
dogs race unleashed through greenery

or scavenge ownerless in fog
emerging on the first warm day.

After the Recent Unpleasantness

Don't take this the wrong way but
maybe given everything, given what
remains — how much, how many more —
it wouldn't kill you to consider
dancing, just this once, alone
in backyard secrecy while dawn
arrays dishevelled underclothes.
Then neighbors grab binoculars, behold
slow pirouettes through sprinkler mist,
jetés across damp grass and whisper *Jesus Christ
he's lost it should we call, should we
make sure he's okay?*

                Or should we join,
awakened from malignant spell
extend numb arms to touch
forbidden hands and lips again,
feet bare, legs flexible as boughs
alive with muscle memory.
And if authorities object
so what, let commuters late for trains
jump in as chanting children count and turn
their rope beneath quick feet,
let garden gnomes transform
to dervishes and whirl
reborn, and let the sleepless
be absolved from vigilance,
find diurnal rhythm in held breath

exhaled and deeply drawn because
this dance keeps time,
immense but delicate,
revolving atmospheres and stars
as dew depends from amaryllis scapes
until the sun, made ravenous,
consumes each trembling globe —
your legacy,
for now.

III. The Underpass

Search

The wistful prophets of apocalypse
rue better times, when drought and summer snow
defied our experts' weather almanacs.
Believers flocked on hills to pray, eclipsed
beneath the livid, funerary sky
that silenced every animal and bird.
Nowadays the eye requires another
eye; passive witness doesn't satisfy.
We click through messages to buy, arrive
on pages sensing we're remote observed,
ills diagnosed and passions data-mined
more deeply than we excavate ourselves.
Like travellers departing from a train
we stumble forth on unfamiliar ground,
beset by furtive men who offer anything
you want, whatever, oxy, DOA,
you looking for a girl, okay, a boy,
it's dangerous without a guide because
you shouldn't be alone tonight, my friend.

For the Foreseeable

It isn't if but when enough
runs dry, the riverbed a flume of stones
still damp when overturned. Undone
by circumstantial evidence you bluff

until confronted with debris,
forgetting how words folded in upon
themselves, an origami crane,
where contradictions needed to agree.

Doesn't matter how decisions
happened; conspiring memories remove
each inconvenient fact to prove
whatever fiction marries means to ends.

So houses burn, a total loss
insurance compensates to raise again.
So summer's a comparison,
the hottest since, more arid than, the worst.

You wonder where it ends: Alone
beneath a bush somewhere, inside a nest,
this darkened room, preparedness
a lamp against whatever finds you when?

Migration

October dawn, another day to kill
before narcotic darkness fastens down.
Within my sleeping bag's black chrysalis

I wake, break camp, by headlamp find the trail
ascending into sun along the ridge.
A man positions tripods facing north

northeast across the scenic overlook.
Traversing thermoclines alone, in pairs,
hawks vault through limpid corridors of air

above the height of land. He photographs
each cool indifferent gaze, flared wings and tail,
efficient talons clenched on senseless prey.

My wife died seven years ago today,
he calls familiarly. *We followed them
until her blood tests came. Stage 3, then 4,*

*so fast we hardly had the chance to say
goodbye. I don't know what I'm doing here
or why — if nothing else it's easier.*

*They're beautiful, but cold; no greed or guilt.
I've seen enough to know we're second hand
to them, not real, beneath attending to.*

They leave, devour, return to breed — that's it.
Our little lives could be invisible
for all they care. I hear him out, polite,

dysphoric as a priest concealed from those
he serves, who listens to forgive without
authority. All ears, a vessel filled

and emptied by parishioners of shame,
resentment, doubt, indelicate desire.
He asks my name and phone number, email.

Confused, our shared experience too frail,
I make apologies and turn away,
abandon him to predators our kin

fed entrails to, ambassadors for gods
that still inhabited a secret world
through which all pass from pain, bound souls released,

companion pets and food to nourish us
in arid lands and dripping labyrinths
beyond the touch of light, forgetful, blind,

evolving as we flee until remade,
unrecognizable but sentient,
no longer hungering for who we loved.

Apnea

By doors kept dark and cool to ease
safe passageway   cool sulphur air
upwells from lakes no living eye's
beheld   sharp tugs prick follicles
hair raised in ancient reflex   *Now*
anus   nostrils   inner ear   brow
and groin   tear ducts   tongue   anywhere
the body's furred or inside out
revenants exchange themselves   theirs
through overhang and kettle hole
abandoned trestle   drainage ditch
mud slick of low tide meadowlands
ours one by one on stairwells when
we falter   fallen off   on trains
presumed asleep by cleaning crews
in ergonomic office chairs
familiar rooms   without a trace
adrift   lost messengers between
deliveries   unquiet breaths
exhaled but never taken in

Easy Way Out

It really would be better if they died,
the olds, still cognizant, beloved yes
but honestly? Like curdled milk or meat
left out they linger past the sell-by date,
disguised by scarves and matching turtlenecks;
or silently endure in shuttered space
until their boat departs for darker shores.
Better they escape at night, one by one,
subsiding out of sight and mind, alone —
no will and testament, no posthumous
reward or clothes to bag for charity —
and leave the way they nakedly arrived
through doors unmarked by grief, bequeathing us
the cold, deep solace of an empty house.

The Harrower

A ditch parts husks of villagers.
Pale bodies heaped for prompt disposal, spent.
A boy approaches, fleeing hell
suspiciously well-fed
(as commentators later note).
Bright eyes and healthy teeth
suggest the photo's staged, composite hoax
where past and present tense
elide. What child
could pass through slaughter unaware?
And yet they do;
he did, and we must too.
That's the path forgetful orphans
take, our parents gone before we knew
enough to harvest memory
against the day such cells
devour themselves. Riding air, we travel
light between this world and theirs,
reluctant guests, malinger
where they were.
               That boy:
He lived anonymous, a workingman,
identified through ledger notes
his captors kept meticulous,
each name a number, date, and means
of end. Not one

spared but he, whose record line
concluded blank and left
the question open. Nor when found,
now smalltown widowed pensioner,
and dogged by press could he recall
who framed and shot his one surviving proof
or where he wandered next or why
he seemed to smile or what,
before, he fed
upon.

The Way Back

Not pebbles   bread   abandoned children's shoes
scat trail of fearful ingenuity
but contour lines   familiar sloping hills
crushed mailbox where we know to turn   don't tell
light falling as it fell across the lake
in postcard photographs   our neighbor seemed
grandfatherly   side door so dark and low
outsiders wouldn't dare investigate
we scavenged garbage   basements   backyard sheds
for private implements   with crows convened
on autumn roads to pluck remains and scream
no telling where we ended up or who
pursued   the glazed and crenellated house
the oven's rancid breath   don't tell how close
we came or what we did to live again
air parting air   we glide enshadowed paths
malingering among regretful things
damp pebbles bright as eyes   crusts soft and warm
our shoes transparent   delicate   they fit
as if we never ran away   unlaced
deranged   splayed open with their tongues pulled out

The Plunge Pool

So many fly
or fall from beam and windowsill,
arms flared, thighs pedalling to claw
ascent from air. Sheer cliff
behind the scenic overlook,
escarpment, trestle, ladder set aslant,
vaulting bridge and gothic spire,
fifth level of the parking deck,
lost pyramids of global capital.
Flying free, by whirling gale
exhaled, centrifugal
derailment of packed rollercoaster cars
forgiven by consent: God's will.
And everywhere in plucked out fields,
from rooftop vents to powerlines
stoop crows that usher things along.

You open closets redolent
with cigarettes and Friday fish:
sweater bags, outdated slacks,
bras hung like skins on drying racks,
pajamas and frayed underwear
no charity accepts. For who
will wear the raiments of the dead?
Or pass undampened through the river
cut between high ledges where
initiates stripped bare
climb cairns of scree, hesitate
above the black, propitiatory pool,
then follow down.

What Doesn't Kill You

The backyard copperhead
decapitated.

Stair edge and running fall,
indented skull

blood-dark at fifty nine.
Ammonia mixed with basement turpentine.

Yellowjacket nest
disturbed by careless feet, pall of dust

on furniture and ragweed pollen silting air,
frail ligatures

wound patiently on throat, through swollen
lungs enflamed by histamines.

Knife keen in humid subway underworld,
furled

bills the obol granting passage.
Infection. Hemorrhage.

Heart fibrillating on the windowsill:
systole absent diastole.

Cool shadow cast, withdrawn.
A sense of something immanent but gone.

Undiagnosed collapse
until the pocket mirror glass

no longer fogs before the mouth and quiet
seals its lid and light,

which lingers last, abandons eyes by slow degree,
then — utterly.

The Hatch

That sound   that midnight thrum and hush
alive   electric   fillings drilled
compressed by anesthesia   pain
a ledge beneath which ledges fall
away   cicada radios
control your private frequency
cull information   auto-fill
before it's clear what's being asked
hacker gods   phishers after souls
or credit cards   whatever's worth
anonymous repurposing
impossible to know who's who
when everyone's displayed   disguised
by user name   no alias
too false to breach security
the smartest person in the room's
the room   there's nothing you can't say
or won't reveal   you follow   lurk
between assumed identities
in parallel   apparelled in
transparency   are followed home
by sound   enormous   strobed   a drone
crescendo hovering above
your bed to hear its listener
exhale   breath rasps as if through mud
tinnitus louder than the din
you cannot hear to think   so sleep
clench eyes and ears against the dark
as children sought by reavers will
to be unheard   invisible

Process of Elimination

The soft implosion of an elder giving way
disturbs the holiday.

Commotion through euonymus;
one scream, extinguished.
An ambulance arrives, removes, departs.
No rush.

White scattered quills, debris of war.
Look Dad, a feather star!

Within the bearing wall plump bees —
wetnurses of forgetfulness —
unbind beam and library.
Even the eaves surrender to such care.

The specialist rules out, each test
eliminating ifs until the then.

Din of trucks across the iron bridge
cannot deter the cool
relentless voice inquiring why
you loiter in the underpass?

Theirs

No-one left knows where
it opens in.
               Now overgrown,
behind a rise where limestone
crumbles under layered shale
the entrance hollows
wide enough to hide a child,
then beckons down.
                       On hands and knees
in headlamp glow the tunnel
coils as if it held some larval thing,
which fed for secret centuries
inside this caul
                 to change, unfurl, and fly.
Deeper on the way's
confused by branching humid passages
where water seeps and ebbs,

                           a throat
with room to stride along,
to urge reluctant pilgrims *hush,*
we're almost there, a little more ...
Spread hand and fingerprints on gutted walls,
red backpack gnawed to thread,
sneaker sole and pencil case
like reliquary shards.

                      Who beheld these
didn't talk or leave a paper trail.
The map of burial
erodes with air and age,
as time-lapse photographs reveal
beneath a fallow onion field
stone circle, cistern, mound and pit
of blackened bone, their sacraments
dispersed for newer blood,
though no-one left knows where.

The Angler

I fish upriver through forgetful hours.
New light becomes mid-afternoon, then dusk.
Line furls and hisses over eddy pools,
behind rip-rap and tumbledown debris.

At once trout rise to sip the evening hatch.
I step into a hollow deeply cold,
flat surface black and perfect, undefiled.
Beyond peripheries a gnawing roar

crescendos louder with approach: Horseflies
circle someone unfamiliar, who casts
precise to ten and noon and two and four
as if enforcing time. Face hidden by

torn veils of shade the angler stills and spreads
what look like wings, a predatory bird's.
Across the swell I call a cautious truce:
You fish your side and I'll fish mine, okay?

Declining answer or acknowledgement
he quadrant casts until invisible,
the only sound his swarming retinue
of eyes and mouths that summon darkness on,

obscuring every path. Direction spins
awry; the flies unsettle, fasten down.
I back away and turn reluctantly
to run, soft steps behind, before, beside,

breath thick with rotten leaves and soil, each feint
encircled by implacable pursuit,
a patient knowingness that waits me out
until, surrendering, I bare my neck.

I

It works like this:
You whisper low enough to lure
one listener, who wanders close
reluctantly and shy.
                      A wave
arriving over space and time,
transformed by minute bone and hair
across the auditory nerve to voice
unrecognized by satellites, beneath
surveillance tools and server farms.
Star tone, anomalous.
                      From there
it moves, breath kindling breath,
flame flame, embodied as it flows
invisibly through leaves
while watchful birds go still
as if a predator draws near.
                      And when
it's done, host flensed and gnawed to bone
discarded over fields the crows patrol,
our heirs will marvel how it happened,
why we acquiesced —
an immanence or spell
possessing us, claim laid
without informed consent —
the only evidence this glyph
inscribed on every door and wall,
dread alphabet of one
forgotten but alive,
your language buried under ice and peat,
in dripping caverns made complete,
written to be heard.

Friends and Acquaintances

One cuts her throat from ear to ear
witnessed by the bathroom mirror,
dismaying bridge and tennis friends

who feel accused. Another points
his parents' Cadillac DeVille
toward oblivion downhill,

the ancient landmark elm he T-
bones mourned in headline eulogy:
Suicide Dooms Historic Tree.

A neighbor doubles down against
professionals he cannot pay
and kneels to take the consequence.

The girl who cigarettes her thighs.
The pond across the street from school
that little faggot's thrown into.

Shades pulled, anonymous, his house
a careful bachelor's domain
attracting us with promises:

cold beer and harder stuff, tv,
his patient and persuasive need.
He knows exactly who we are.

Whereabouts Unknown

He lies as if already carved in stone:
cold brow, patrician nose and chin, clasped palms
expecting swift ascent to cloudy realms.
No fearful penitence for what he'd done.
Anonymous, the hospice room erased
remains of circumstantial evidence.
Here predators enjoy beneficence,
abluted, powdered, turned, and fed with grace.
Rough justice would ignore these rituals,
deny iniquity should find reprieve
with constant laying on of hands. Soft bells
suggest it's time for visitors to leave.
Forgiven trespass, he demurs with tact,
I'd rather not get into all of that.

Darkling

It's over now, my secret's safe with you.

The reason doesn't matter anymore;
we're long since past forgiveness to forget.

Whatever happened happened in between:
underpass and median, scavenged lot,
safe dumping ground of spit and meadowlands.

Rehearsing lies in case occasion rose
I didn't tell, until one broken word
betrayed our trust with indiscreet recall
too quick and candid to escape.

                              Some nights
you circle closer, soft enormous moth
pursuing flame, drawn in, ignited, spent.

Black abdomen and wings occlude my eyes.

They tear to rinse away the residue.

Exit Interview

Where are you going?   *Nowhere worth knowing.*

What are you taking?   *Nothing worth owning.*

Who will protect you?   *No-one but strangers.*

Will you forget me?   *Never or later.*

Why?   *You know better than I to confess.*

Can you bear complicity alone?   *Yes.*

IV. As Is

Totems

Head bowed, great shoulders hulls
beneath loose skin and silver fur,
Ursus arctos horribilis
prowls his cage's scant perimeter.
It's hot, we're starved, there's not enough to do.
This scabby weekend zoo's
a nursing home for ruined gods. Potties
occupied, redolent with us,
we bypass one-winged predatory birds,
blind wolf and flyblown chimpanzee
back turned, contemptuous.

The placard's educational.
Orphaned as a cub (his mother's trophy
snarls beside the ticket desk
like life, we read aloud), Pee Wee
learned to somersault and pratfall,
beg, simper, prance an awkward minuet.
He toured state fairs with sideshow acts,
freaks, firewalkers, acrobats,
delighting children of all ages,
Tyrolean hat and vest too small
for such appendages.

Leaning on her tripod cane,
left side dead weight,
Mom stands before the cage and smokes Pall-Malls.
We shout "Hey Pee Wee! Over here!"
taunting for a glance, one roar
recordable on film.
She mutters to him under breath,
curse or invocation,
then limps away from what she wrought, her kin —
wide eyed and gaping, strange with glee —
abandoned for the parking lot.

Oblivious, he circles ceaselessly.
Our voices dwindle, still.
Without quite knowing why we yank
kids' hands and unacknowledged flee
as if from something freed,
damp breath inhabiting our pores.
The exit's weathered wooden Indian
guards between dimensions,
palm up in greeting or farewell,
permission or reproach,
no telling which.

Nightlight

In her kitchen, after school,
Mom comforted us and said,
Don't bury your light.

But when her blue
unblinking eyes go out
we thumb them fast,

abashed, as if she knows
our touch upon each one
and wonders why we rush to blind our dead?

Scab

Ardent for experience it
penetrates: god or fugitive,
embodied echo, midday light
made keen through magnifying lens.
Past ossicle and cilia,
frail doormen to the inner ear,
disorienting rod and cone
it floods the brain and harbors there
enhived, a queen awaiting kin.
Impossible to quantify,
familiar alien, one cell
metastasizing secretly
behind the union picket line.
Will work for food, for anything
you own — first leftovers and spare
potatoes, apples, cellar roots —
then cash, then working capital,
walls stripped to studs and fixtures sold
for scrap, and finally takes breath,
whets tender parts to skin and bone
but leaves the coroner to probe
this kiss, coagulated from
regret and misbegotten love
for having wholly known you when.

Afield

When you ascend from coma
wakening, these lucid minutes
given back in bed, we witness
science and common sense belied
by stranger truth.
                        Voice bold and clear,
no longer rasped oracular
through blackened lungs. Eyes keen,
igniting as you name
those here and gone, and memory
emergent from its mute cocoon
to fill and glisten in the hospice room's
fluorescent dawn.
                        The modest Denver home
ploughed under office tower blocks
sprouts whole, back patio wherein you smoked
deliciously alone before
My Antonia and *O Pioneers!*
and weekends herding Alpine goats
off ledge and outcropped stone,
your aunt's redoubt a secret cleft
between existences. Each stalk
bore dew, and stands of aspen
rattled in one voice, immense
but soft, inaudible to all
save you.

      So when a pause
extends from breath to taking leave
and silence fastens down
I hope you find what we imagine there:
Mist rising from the lower valleys as
you wander unencumbered by regret
while gentle creatures and companions move
aside in unison and ease your way
to farther fields, wherever you may go.

Rise

Next time you die don't bother me,
okay? It's hard enough to say
goodbye without repeating that tableau,
dark bed a boat adrift,
our hands like lines untethered, letting go.
Each breath calls off the last, another, pause —.
Before your body cools we brush
eyes shut and straighten limbs to ease
disposability
with semblances of peace.
Maybe you'll return, egg or embryo,
glistening as roe, garden grub,
anonymous in cloudy hatch
or named, delivered whole,
aware you lived and seeking us
on paths that might not cross
this go around. We'll meet
near intersections safe
for revenants to enter through:
The kettle pond beneath thick fog
unseen by anyone,
and where your shadow lifts to sip
one mayfly from the brim
a circle opens, widening.

Lighting Up

Bring me back across spacetime   complete
from quark and gluon   plasma   heat
compressed through black holes in reverse
so galaxies expand and stars
ignite the awful chandelier
my backyard telescope drew near.

Bring summer afternoons again
cool shadows under oak and elm
forsythia to hide within
sunken palaces beneath damp slate
and roses trellised in recumbent humming aisles
no gaze could violate.

From the upright out-of-tune piano
long silenced   dusty from disuse
let large expressive fingers draw
sonatas   nocturnes   calm etudes
before kids clatter in from school
destroy the spell   her voice inaudible.

Don't forget the lost   discarded   killed and kept
stray hairpins   orphaned shoes   lighters drained of fuel
fossils   hives and plundered nests
pinned butterflies above reptilian bones
the line of wrack from tides withdrawn
moon gone   never to return.

And when I wake from restless dream
where space collapsed in one enormous breath
to painted dinosaurs and planets
hung in makeshift orrery
then tiptoe from my boyhood room
and crane around the kitchen door to see

her   bring my mother respite and return
coffee steaming on the yellow windowsill
before she opens curtains to the sun
requites the early calls of doves and cardinals
and flicking down the flywheel button lights
the day's first menthol-cool   delicious   cigarette.

Night Swimming

Midsummer, wind across the lake
the humid morning breath of thunderheads.
Too small for awkward jutting oars
I rowed in futile circles, out of synch.
My boat heaved broadside whitecap waves,
near swamped; both oarlocks tore from sockets, gone.
Adrift, embarrassed and undone
I wept until you dove with lifeguard's grace,
precise swift strokes and scissor kicks
that found a mooring line to draw me in.

The verge spreads black and calm, immense.
I'm far beyond familiar lakefront homes.
My wake's erased itself; low clouds,
no star or moon to reckon bearing by
nor voice encouraging from shore.
All night you leap across the boundary
and swim me down but water pulls
again, again, an awful knowingness
so cold you gasp and lunge to touch
this hand I reach with, grasping only air.

Bearing Wall

A crack runs vertical — *uh oh*.
My wife inclines one cautionary brow.
White pine floorboards bow downhill,
slow sedimental flow
beneath foundation stones. Last line
against collapse this wall
resists encroaching gravity and time
with honeycombs of lath, plaster
cladding over beams and columns
braced by hand. *Good bones*,
the broker offers hopefully,
white lie to gild the obvious.

I see again the curtained bed
we stood around, stoic but adrift.
Our mother lay half-conscious,
flush with metastatic cancer,
every bone a hive the CAT scan
mapped like valleys of the moon.
She'd fallen hard, a broken thigh;
we couldn't bear to tell her this was it.
Unaware, *just dropping by*,
the orthopaedist planned to operate.
My brother cursed and left the room.

Now I trace another fracture
floor to ceiling, back again,
feel years of weight
compressed behind, immense —
a family's inheritance —
push out. *We'll let you know*
I say, and like that surgeon's face
the broker's sags, admitting false
pretence: What's ruined cannot stay
or be repaired, it's gone,
a knockdown, total loss,
as when she stirred awake and groaned
I'm done with this
and everything gave way.

Visiting Hours

Crossing homeward at the traffic light
impatience roars behind. Torn loose
I follow birds, provisioning for night.

EMTs affix a spinal brace.
Cool fingertips anointing elbows, face,

prepare a vein where slow
millennia of silt collect.
Sensation dulls below

my waist, then neck, narcotic tide
to heal and purify

rude flesh and ease its errant path
through time. Familiar warmth
insinuates my groin — our childhood cat,

Mom's avatar — and kneads with claws
withdrawn, adept in common cause.

From vents and air conditioners
she drifts, pale caul,
forbidden fuck-you cigarette dispersed

again, restoring realm.
What cannot be a palm

assays my brow for evidence.
I wrench awake, cry out —
too near a boundary of sense

beyond which few return
coherent or unburned.

On call the evening nurse appears,
inhales suspiciously.
What's wrong? Who's smoking here?

All innocence, I lie:
No worries. Why?

Cemetery Geese

Absurd, obscene —
plump bottoms canted on parade,
bills in avid unison
adeptly plucking blade by blade
around worn cenotaphs and plinths,
meticulous as priests accounting sin.
The graveyard slicks with excrement
when waves descend, install
their raucous parliament
against the chime of Sunday service bells.
With bristle brush and Windex spray
I kneel before my mother's mottled stone.
Beneath her name, as lichen peels away,
the petals of a rose emerge;
dull granite brightens like a swollen door
eased open.
               One goose steps near,
unsettlingly familiar.
Intent, she holds my eye
the way my mother prosecuted lies;
we stare each other down.
Fuck off, I mutter under breath, ashamed.
In regal dignity she turns
to graze adjacent plots.

                        Then sudden rush —
as if by prearranged consent
all launch in an embodiment,
broad pinions flared and thrumming while they rise
in skeins behind a lead,
drafting wakes and currents, organized
so each surrenders to another's call
for more abundant fields
and summoned, yields.

As Is

We list your home as is,
ghost ship uncaptained by disease,
slow mutinies of stuff.
Ash-pocked couch, bottom-broken chair
compressed by bridge and cocktail Saturdays,
glossy mahogany antique
beneath cheap bric-a-brac.
Three childhood beds pristine, four-poster where
you dreamed, made life, and blinked goodbye.

Ignore the broker's plea
for curb appeal; no autumn mums and mulch,
no windows washed or touch-up paint,
no grout to seal the yellowed clawfoot tub
you bathed us in, initiates,
smooth bodies perfect bowls. Not one
concession to a buyer's proud
entitlement. We loom
aloof, immoveable in rooms

where pregnant couples mime distaste,
gesticulate and pout,
presumptive heirs, each crack and faucet drip
announced against the price.
Swollen frame and cabinets mis-hung, brush
to prune and runneled driveway pave,

moss-damp roof, ancient boiler jerry-rigged
until we glare them out,
regretful, exiled, looking back.

Unsold as seasons toll, the lawn
goads neighbors to complain. We trim and weed,
shovel, rake, air and put away.
Windex, Clorox, Black Flag, Lysol,
Pledge and Bon Ami. Merit cigarettes
in cellophane, still fresh.
Faint essences inhaled
you linger near, companionable shades
assuming rightful place.

The broker quits, commissionless.
We watch her ease from the corroding stoop,
depointed bricks like wayward teeth.
Inside, the bevelled foyer glass
(*So tacky*, whispered guests)
returns our likenesses but strangely dim,
too long beheld to compass space
or time. Dominion ours,
inheritors, we bolt the door.

The Boathouse Swallows

Late March, against their annual return,
    my brother and I clip
thick tarp along the gaping boathouse door
    and ratchet shut until
        the skirt's submerged.
  Denied, the swallows circle patiently.
Next week our jerry-rigging fails;
    stiff wind across the lake
    unzips and rends it free,
       surrendering.

They enter then, a mated pair
from forebears christened there
    in nests too high to broom.
We clap and shoo, evacuate
our property, scrub out the spattered boat
    besieged by sneak attack.
     Relentless, sleek,
    wings fletched for speed and aim
      they vector down
surprise fly-by's and rend pale thinning scalps.

    Disarmed by grace we curse,
        abandon ship.
    Mom's laughter fills our ears —
  rasp and knowing cackle, pungent

    cigarette — long distance echo
        sent years ago
across forgotten scenic overlooks.
She loved this futile sibling comedy,
        raw nature thwarting men
        determined to expel

    what cannot be.
They'll never stop, they'll find a way.
Why you bother is beyond me.
    Her birds replied by name,
approaching where she knelt alone and spoke
familial tongues inscrutable to all
    but them. Now swallows flock,
    surrounding us as if they hear
        an absent voice
        and follow on its frequency.

    The door won't hold.
    This house will be inhabited
    by souls mysterious to ours,
        executors and heirs,
boat feather-strewn and filthy prow to stern.
    New generations navigate
        unerringly
by markers only visible from air,

as someday we prepare
departure, never doubting route

to final origin,
and with our own begin
circumferences of descent above
another lake at dusk,
inscribing mist
exhaled by calm cool water while we feed
together on the mayfly hatch
in what our former species once
imagined appetite,
but we call joy.

Acknowledgements

Thank you to the editors of the following journals, where some of these poems were first published:

Antioch Review: "The Way Back"

Atlanta Review: "Found"

Coachella Review: "The Harrower"

Five Points: "Easter Candles," "Totems," and "The Plunge Pool"

Hollins Critic: "Nightlight"

Hopkins Review: "Host" and "Process of Elimination"

New York Quarterly: "Who What When Where Why"

Nimrod: "As Is"

Passengers: "Search" and "Bellfounding"

Poetry Northwest: "The Hatch"

Redactions: "The Angler"

This Broken Shore: "Carriers," "Empties," "Overheard," and "Touch and Go"

The Yale Review: "Night Swimming"

Vox Populi: "After the Recent Unpleasantness"

West Trade: "Trestle Jumping"

About the Author

George Witte is the author of three previous collections: *The Apparitioners*, *Deniability*, and *Does She Have a Name?* His poems have been published in a range of journals and anthologized in *The Best American Poetry*, *Old Flame*, *Rabbit Ears*, *The Doll Collection*, and *Poets of the Palisades*. He received *Poetry* magazine's Frederick Bock prize, as well as a fellowship from the New Jersey Council for the Arts. A New Jersey native and career book editor, he lives with his family in Ridgewood, New Jersey.

About the Type and Paper

Designed by Malou Verlomme of the Monotype Studio, Macklin is an elegant, high-contrast typeface. It has been designed purposely for more emotional appeal.

The concept for Macklin began with research on historical material from Britain and Europe dating to the beginning of the 19th century, specifically the work of Vincent Figgins. Verlomme pays respect to Figgins's work with Macklin, but pushes the family to a more contemporary place.

This book is printed on natural Rolland Enviro Book stock. The paper is 100 percent post-consumer sustainable fiber content and is FSC-certified.

An Abundance of Caution was designed by Eleanor Safe and Joe Floresca.

Unbound Edition Press champions honest, original voices. Committed to the power of writers who explore and illuminate the contemporary human condition, we publish collections of poetry, short fiction, and essays. Our publisher and editorial team aim to identify, develop, and defend authors who create thoughtfully challenging work which may not find a home with mainstream publishers. We are guided by a mission to respect and elevate emerging, under-appreciated, and marginalized authors, with a strong commitment to advancing LGBTQ+ and BIPOC voices. We are honored to make meaningful contributions to the literary arts by publishing their work.

unboundedition.com